Granny Square Crochet Patterns Made Easy

Make Decorative Crochet Stitches and Motifs with this Beginner's Guide to Contemporary Granny Squares

By

Zera Meyer

Disclaimer

This book offers knowledgeable and trustworthy information on the subject area discussed. Nevertheless, the opinions presented in this work belong solely to the author and are not intended to be considered expert advice or counsel. The reader is therefore accountable for his/ her own decision.

Contents

Introduction

Who among you started your crocheting journey by making granny squares? Well, I sure did. I clearly recall embarking on a family road trip with my sister and mom and having to pass out time crocheting granny squares in several patterns. It was such a fun and pleasant way of being opportune to learn several crochet patterns and stitches. When I got tired of one stitch, I could simply proceed with the next square because the squares worked up beautifully and easily. These squares ultimately got joined to become a large afghan. Granny Squares are incredibly satisfying to crochet because they come together so quickly. It takes only a short amount of time to make several of them.

Granny squares can be used for more than just crocheting afghans or blankets. These granny squares are excellent for shawls, patchwork, purses, scarves, and pillowcases, among many others. You can also crochet a completely different appearance by switching your yarn color or stitch. The possibilities are endless!

Getting Started

What is a Granny Square?

A granny square is one of the most basic and simplest crochet motifs in the crocheting craft, which are a well-liked choice for new crocheters just learning the different crochet stitches available since they're very simple and quick to create.

Granny squares are formed using basic crochet stitches, such as double crochet stitch, slip stitch, and chain stitch, and are simple to identify by their shape and look, typically in the form of square and lace. Granny squares are a fantastic approach to using up pieces of yarn scraps since they're often small in size and can be made in a single solid color or with a separate color of yarn for every round. Upon completing a few granny squares, you could join them to create bigger items such as sweaters, blankets, scarves, crochet, afghan, and other simple crochet patterns.

It's quite unclear where the name **"Granny Squares"** came from. According to a common myth, grandmothers who were unable to assist with physical labor or other domestic chores made garments and blankets for their families out of various pieces of fabric. Given the granny square patterns are ideal for using up scraps of yarn, they were given the moniker "Granny Squares" because grandmas frequently find satisfaction in making them.

Method of Construction

The center of a granny square is worked first, proceeding outward. The squares are worked in connected rounds while using a slip stitch to close up every round. The rounds are made of a repetitive pattern of motifs.

For instance, to create the classic granny square motif, you will use the double crochet cluster, or the granny clusters, consisting of 3 DCs (double crochet) made within the same space/ gap. A ch-1 space separates the granny clusters along the sides and ch-3 spaces at the square's 4 corners.

Variations

There are numerous patterns or motifs for granny squares. The classic and solid are two really simple variations. There're different kinds of flower variations, such as daisies and sunflowers. Also, there is the 3D stacked granny square variation, which can be used in creating many granny squares in the form of hexagons and triangles. More of these granny square variations will be covered in later sections of this book.

Essential Supplies

Crochet Hook

Different sizes are available for crochet hooks. The most common size for beginner/new crocheters is size H or 5mm. Several yarn producers label their yarns with the recommended size of hook that it's best to work with, so look for these labels when shopping for crochet hooks.

How your hook feels is another factor to take into account. Most handles for hooks are ergonomic and simpler to handle, so test them and assess which one is most convenient for you.

Yarn

The ability to use any yarn, from heavy wool to lightweight cotton, is one lovely thing about granny squares. Everything relies on the style you want to achieve. Granny squares can be made entirely out of a single color or several yarns if you want to have multiple colors. Also, you would not want to be overwhelmed in the beginning stage, so get a yarn whose color is bright so you can see well enough when making your granny square.

Additionally, as a beginner, go for the worsted weight yarn (#4) or double-knit yarn (#3). These bulkier yarn types will be much easier to handle when you first start off before moving on to more complex work in crocheting. For the best results in your granny square project, ensure the same weight of yarn is used all through.

Hint:

Use a self-striping or multicolored yarn if you'd like your granny square to feature a great deal of color without having to join fresh yarn strands. With a multicolored yarn, everything is pretty done for you, and the result will be a stunning square with several different colors.

Tapestry Needles

These big eye needles are used in sewing ends to give your squares a polished appearance. You may need a few different sizes depending on the yarns you have decided on.

Extra Notions

Scissors

You'll require a pair of scissors to snip your yarn. Most crocheters prefer keeping a small but lovely pair of scissors nearby.

Stitch Markers/ Safety Pins

They are good at holding your work in place while you plan and join several granny squares together. You will need stitch markers to mark your stitches in denoting your starting and ending points, thus keeping you on track.

Blocking Mat

Blocking mat is great when you need to block your crochet pieces. Your bed is also an excellent place to block your crochet pieces because it is flat and comfortable.

Basic Crochet Stitches

After you become accustomed to the various stitches, learning to crochet will become a walk in the park. In this section, I will guide you through the fundamental stitches in crochet that you are expected to encounter in all of the granny square patterns in this book. With these fundamental stitches, you can crochet almost any beginner crochet project.

Slipknot

You will always begin with a slipknot regardless of what crochet piece you intend to make. However, this is not considered a stitch but simply how you attach your yarn to your hook to get started with your very first row or ring of stitches.

Steps

1. Create a loop, hooking a different loop across it.

2. Ensure the loop is tightened slightly, then push the knot up into position.

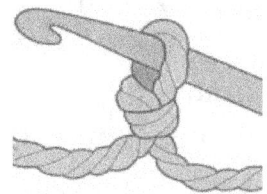

Yarn Over (YO)

For crochet stitches to be made, your yarn must be wrapped around your hook and passed across a pre-existing slipknot or stitch. As a result, each stitch you make will require a yarn over, and some stitches require well over a single yarn over. So practicing this skill is a great thing to do.

Steps

1. With the slipknot on the hook and your working yarn at the back of the hook, the yarn should be wrapped up and across the hook and brought to the forefront of the hook.

2. The working yarn should be pulled across the stitch or knot to create a new stitch by first grabbing the yarn in the hook's crook/ bend. Instead of wrapping the yarn across the hook using your fingers, the hook should be used in grabbing the yarn. The hook should be allowed to do the task. Your crochet stitches will be quicker as a result, and you'll have a uniform tension.

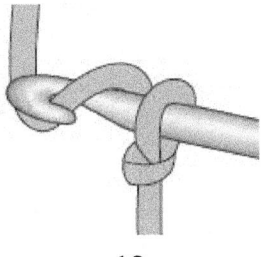

And now, off we go to the main stitches you must practice consistently

Foundation Chain

The foundation chain is where crochet actually begins. A loop must be created on your hook before you can crochet a chain stitch. The foundation chain is then formed by chaining several of the loops or chains of stitches. Typically a crochet pattern would indicate the number of chain stitches needed to form the foundation chain. Afterward, you'd work other stitches into the chain of foundation stitches, like the double or single crochet stitches.

Steps

1. Make a slipknot, yarn over the hook, pulling the yarn across to create a new loop while ensuring not to tighten the existing loop

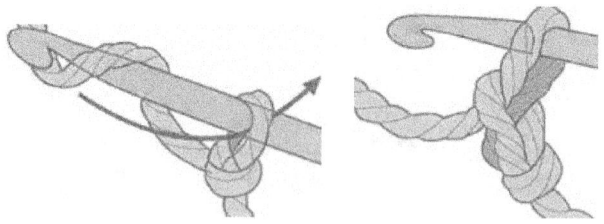

2. The above step should be repeated to create several chain stitches as necessary. A slipknot is not to be counted as a chain stitch.

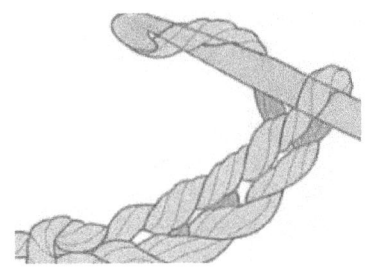

Slip Stitch (Sl St)

One way you can use the slip stitch is when joining your foundation's ends into a circle or ring to crochet in the round like your granny squares (more like joining the last and first stitch of a row to enable you to work in the round).

Alternately, a slip stitch can be used to transfer your hook and working yarn to another location while working without having to cut and rejoin the yarn.

Steps

1. The hook should be inserted into your hook's first chain, from the front to the back.

2. Pass the working yarn from the hook's back through the top. The yarn should be grabbed from the hook's crook/ bend, pulling it across the chain stitch. This will leave your hook with a loop, meaning a stitch has been slipped.

3. The steps above should be repeated till the specified amount of stitches is slipped, as indicated in the project you'd be working on.
4. To work in the round (joining the foundation chain to form a circle), the hook should be inserted into the farthest stitch from the hook, working a slip stitch as previously illustrated

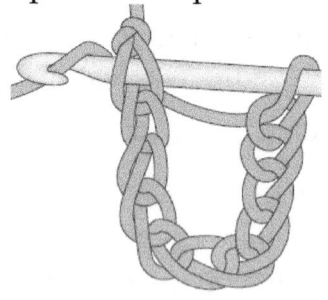

Single Crochet (SC)

Single crochet is often employed in several crochet patterns. Its weave is tighter and shorter than other stitches and is the most popular. Several stitches with closed patterns—those with minimal space between stitches—use single crochet more frequently. It is an excellent stitch for a beginner to learn.

Steps

1. As per usual, create your foundation chain. Then, ensure your work is turned so that you are prepared to continue working on the chain you just created.
2. To begin making a SC, a chain stitch should be skipped; then, the hook should be inserted into the work (the hook's 2nd chain on the foundation chain), bringing the yarn across the chain stitch by yarning over the hook.

3. At this point, 2 loops will be on the hook. After yarning over the hook, it should be pulled across both of its loops.

4. Your hook would be left with a loop; with this, a SC stitch has been made; so congrats.

5. Proceed to work SC all through the foundation chain; work a stitch of SC in every of the other chain stitches

Hint:

Creating SC on successive rows

Upon completing one SC row, chain one (the turning chain), and ensuring your work is turned. At this point, the row that is now completed would not resemble the foundation chain. However, looking carefully, you'd be able to see some stitches recently completed. To complete the successive rows of SC, you can choose to work across the front or the back loop or even a stitch's two loops.

Several crochet patterns typically indicate whether to work across the front loop or the back loop; if there isn't a mention of such, then the two loops should be worked across.

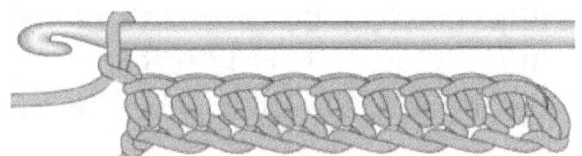

The turning chain should be worked

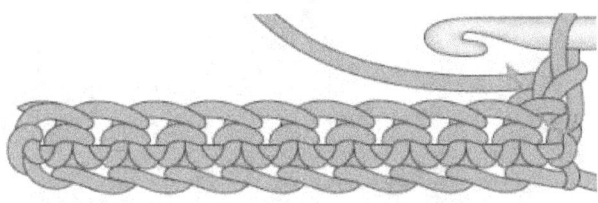

The hook should be inserted beneath the 1st stitch's two loops

Double Crochet (DC)

When compared to a treble crochet stitch, double crochet is considered shorter; however, it is taller compared to single crochet and half double stitches. Fabric created with double crochet stitches is slightly more 'giving' and flexible compared to fabric created from single crochet.

Steps

1. For DC to be worked into a foundation chain, yarn over the hook, skipping 2 or 3 chain stitches (based on if your project pattern requests for 2 or 3 turning chains); then ensure the hook is inserted into the subsequent chain (in the example below, it is the hook's 4th chain from the foundation chain).

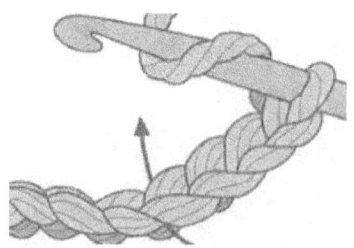

2. Yarn over the hook, pulling it across the chain stitch. Your hook should now have about 3 loops.

19

Yarn over for the second time, pulling the hook across 2 of the hook's loops. Your hook should have 2 loops left on it at this point.

3. Yarn over the hook, pulling it across the hook's last 2 loops. A double crochet stitch has now been made, leaving your hook with a loop.

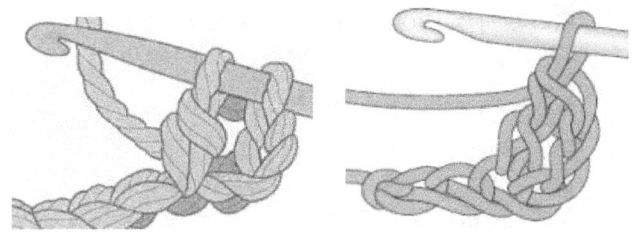

4. Yarn over the hook and ensure the hook is inserted into the subsequent chain stitch, repeating 2 and 3 steps above to add more DC stitches.

Hint:

Creating DC on successive rows

Upon getting to the foundation chain's end for SC, the amount of turning chains needed should be worked; afterward, your work should be turned. Yarn over the hook right into the appropriate section of the stitch (front loop, back loop, or both), working DC stitches through the rows, as illustrated earlier.

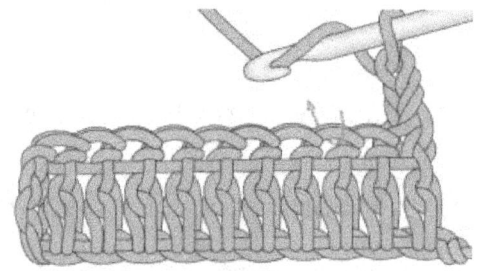

Crocheting row 2 of DC

Half Double Crochet (HDC)

Single crochet (SC) and half double (HDC) crochet stitches are quite comparable. Half double crochet differs because it begins with an additional yarn over. Compared to single crochet, half double crochet is taller as a result of the additional yarn over but shorter compared to double crochet.

Per rigidity and flexibility, half double stitch is midway between SC and DC stitches.

Steps

1. For HDC to be worked into a foundation chain, yarn over the hook, then ensure the hook is inserted into the 3rd chain beginning from the hook/ foundation chain (the chain stitch 1st and 2nd stitches denote the turning chain).

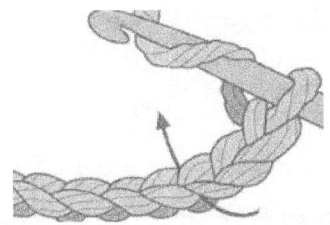

Yarn over the hook once more, pulling the hook across the chain stitch. Your hook should have 3 loops left.

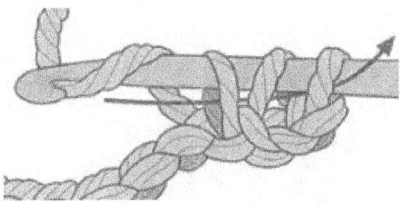

2. Yarn over the hook, pulling across all 3 of the hook's loops. With this, one HDC is completed, leaving your hook with one loop.

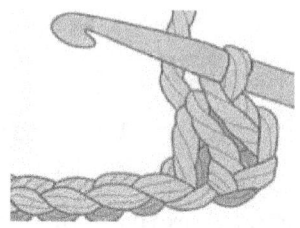

Hint:

Creating HDC on successive rows

Upon getting to the foundation chain's end for SC and DC, the amount of turning chains needed should be worked; afterward, your work should be turned. Yarn over the hook right into the appropriate section of the stitch (front loop, back loop, or both), working HDC stitches through the rows, as illustrated earlier.

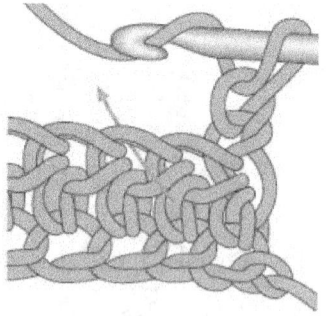

Crocheting row 2 of HDC

Treble Crochet (TR)

Treble (sometimes referred to as triple) crochet is the longest of all other crochet stitches earlier discussed, which produces a fabric with great flexibility and spaces among the stitches.

Steps

1. When working a treble crochet into a foundation chain, ensure to yarn over the hook 2x, bypass chain stitches 1 to 3 or 1 to 4, and have the hook inserted from the front to the back via the foundation chain's subsequent stitch.

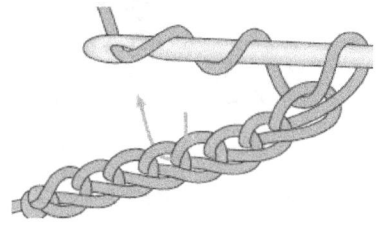

2. Yarn over the hook, and ensure the hook is pulled across the chain stitch (leaving your hook with 4 loops). Yarn over the hook for the second time, and ensure the hook is pulled across two of the hook's loops (leaving your hook with 3 loops).

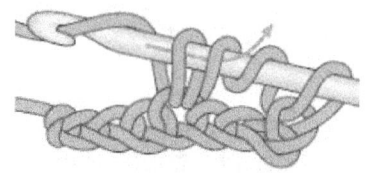

3. Yarn over the hook, and ensure the hook is pulled across two of the hook's loops (leaving your hook with 2 loops). Yarn over the hook again, ensuring the hook is pulled across the other two loops. With this, a treble crochet stitch is completed, leaving your hook with 1 loop.

Starting Off a Granny Square

You can choose a couple of options to start crocheting your granny squares, as treated below.

Method 1: Magic Ring Technique

Magic ring (MR), magic circle (MC), or sometimes called magic loop (M) is a highly helpful technique used to crochet in the round. This is one of my favorites since it gets rid of the annoying gap/ hole that sometimes appears in the middle of my ongoing project. Granny squares, amigurumi, and top-down hat crafts are just a few examples of the many crochet patterns that use magic ring.

Steps

1. Loop Yarn Across Your Fingers

Lay the yarn's tail over the top of your forefinger, working your way from left to right, and then looping it just once over your four fingers. Put the working yarn— the ball end of your skein—behind the yarn's tail end (the yarn's tail end will fall to the left and the working yarn to the right.

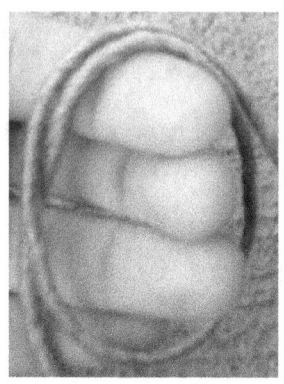

2. Release the Loop

Release the loop from your fingers while the working yarn is kept behind the tail end of the yarn. If it's so laborious to do, use your fingers to hold down/pinch the loop where both yarn strands meet. Pull a loop up from the working yarn using your hook.

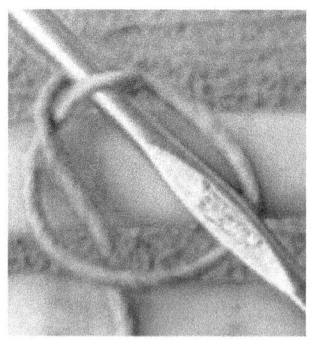

3. Make One Chain (or the specified number of chains)

Ensure the circle of yarn is still in position, wrapping the working yarn through the hook from the back side to the front side. Then pull the yarn across the hook's loop. With this, a chain is completed (this is not considered to be a stitch).

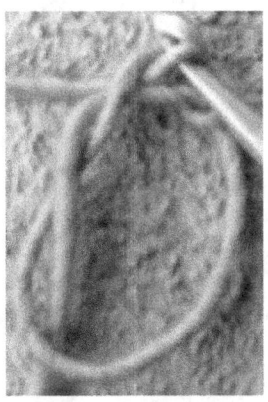

Note: The stitch type employed in the pattern's first round determines how many chain stitches you should make in this step.

- One chain will be made if the pattern begins with a round of SC stitches.

- An additional one chain will be made (making it two chains) if the pattern begins with a round of HDC stitches.
- A total of three chains will be made if the pattern begins with a round of DC stitches.

4. Crochet Stitches into the Ring

Now make a SC across the two yarn strands (the tail of the yarn and the ring).

Proceed to add more SC stitches to the loop till the specified amount of stitches for the pattern has been reached.

5. Close-up the Ring

Use your right-hand fingers to grip your stitches, pulling the yarn tail using your left hand to shut the ring's center.

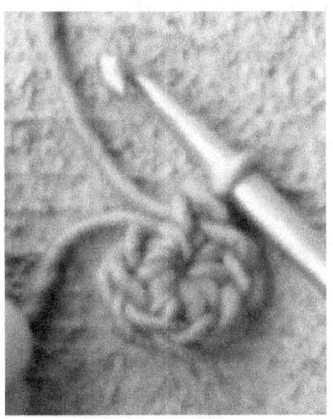

6. Slip Stitch to Finish the Round

A slip stitch should be worked into the first stitch to join the round. Be cautious, so you don't end up stitching into the chain instead of the round's first stitch, then proceed with the pattern

Note: Don't use a slip stitch to join the round if you'll be crocheting in a continual circle. You should rather begin the subsequent round in round 1's first stitch.

A Request from the Author:

Hey, I trust you're having a fascinating read. Please do share your feedback with me!

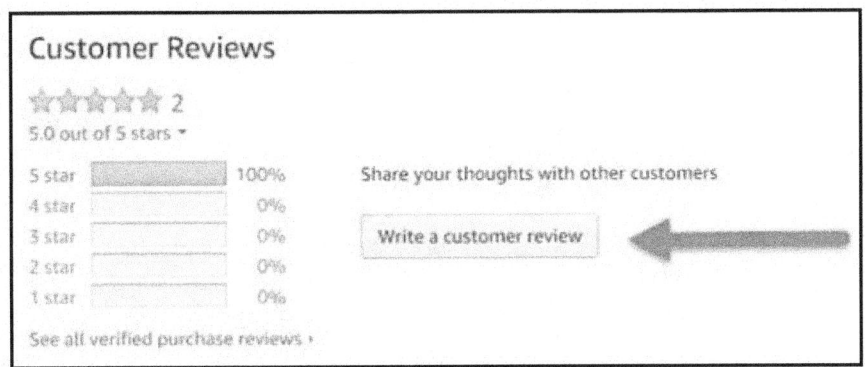

 I'd be forever thankful if you could spend only 60 seconds writing a brief product review of this book on Amazon.

>> To post a brief review, click here.

Thanks so much.

Method 2: Starting in a Single Chain

Steps

1. Chain 4

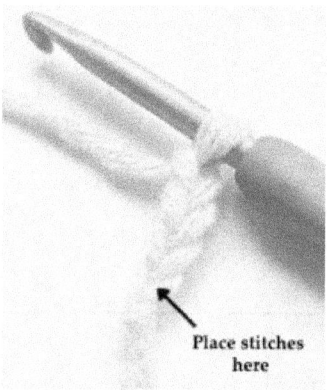

Place stitches here

2. Crochet two DC in the first stitch, then chain 2

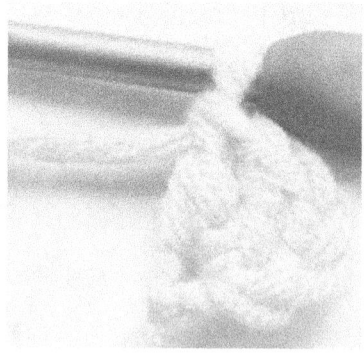

3. Crochet 3 DC, then chain 2. Repeat three times

4. Slip stitch in chain 3's top

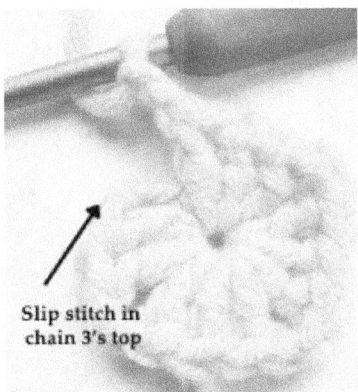

Slip stitch in
chain 3's top

Method 3: Chain Stitching the Center Ring

Steps

1. Chain 4, then slip stitch in the first stitch.

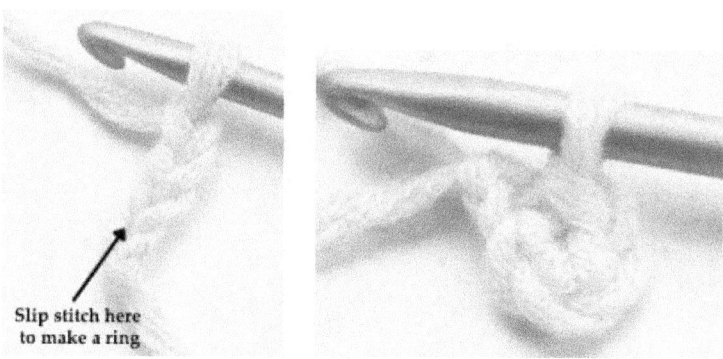

Slip stitch here
to make a ring

2. Chain 3 (this is counted as a DC), crochet two DC in the center ring, then chain 2.

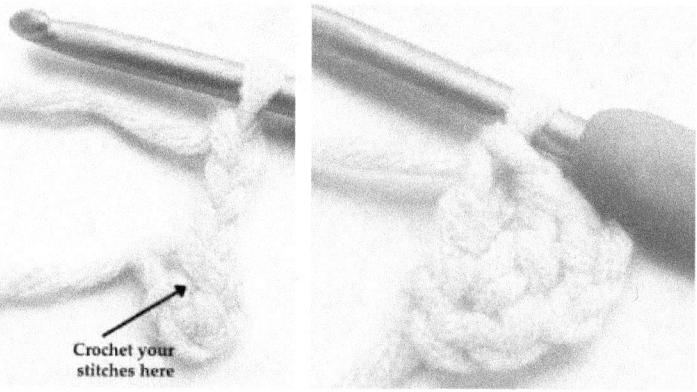

Crochet your
stitches here

3. Make three DC stitches, then chain 2, repeating three times.

4. Slip stitch in chain 3's top

Changing Colors

Granny squares are mostly so vibrant and multicolored in their appearance. Several patterns of granny squares would require you to use a new yarn color when working each round, and most patterns would also require that a new yarn color be joined in the space at the corner. Regardless, below are the steps to introduce a new yarn color to your granny square;

Steps

1. The first yarn color should be used to begin the granny square. After that, the first round's end should be fastened off using the same color you started with.

2. Then change to a different yarn color. A slipknot should be made with your hook using the new yarn.

   The new yarn should then be crocheted onto the granny square. To do this, your hook should be inserted into one of the granny square's corners space (into any chain 2 space).

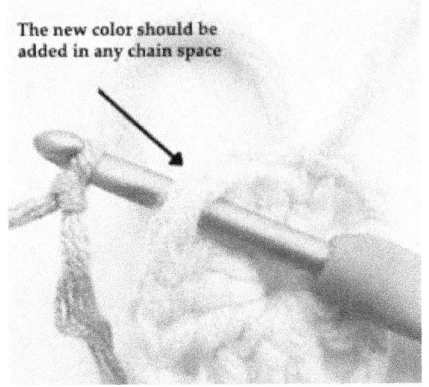

The new color should be added in any chain space

3. A slip stitch should be made by using the new yarn color in yarning over and pulling through. An example is shown below.

4. Then chain 3, or as desired

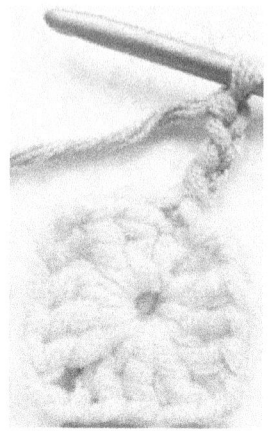

5. At this point, the subsequent round should be worked using the new yarn color.

6. Keep working every round using a new yarn color till you've fulfilled the required number of rounds.

Weaving Your Granny Squares

The final step in completing any crochet piece is to weave in the ends of the yarn. The ends of your yarn must be correctly weaved in to keep your yarn from unraveling with time and to make your work polished and sophisticated.

Why not simply tie a knot instead?

The yarn's ends can be secured with a knot; however, this isn't the ideal way to finish your work. With time, knots may unravel, resulting in uncomfortable rough bumps that wouldn't look good. On the other hand, tightly woven ends are smooth when touched and won't come off easily.

Steps

1. Leave a 6-inch tail of yarn at a minimum after cutting the yarn. The tail of the yarn should then be threaded across your tapestry needle's eye.
2. In the just completed row (last stitches), the yarn should be weaved horizontally across the bases of all the stitches.

3. After that, reverse the direction and use your needle to work some stitches vertically.

4. After that, reverse the direction once more, weaving it across some additional stitches horizontally.

5. Keep at it till all loose ends have been woven in.

Note: If your granny squares uses multiple colors, the ends of the individual yarn color would have to be woven in differently. To make the yarn ends of color A less obvious, weave across the stitches made with the same yarn of color A.

Keeping Your Granny Squares in Shape

One issue about granny squares is that as additional rounds of stitches are added, their corners get curled up, leaving you with a crooked square. This mostly occurs when working in just one direction, which is quite uncomfortable. A crochet item's right and wrong sides will be similar if the turning technique is used. This implies that any side of the granny square can be used since the stitches appear to be evenly clear and distinct.

Blocking your granny squares is another technique that helps to keep your squares in shape. A blocking board and pins made especially for blocking squares can be purchased. But you could also make your own using cardboard, foam mat, or wooden plaques along with chopsticks or pushpins. Wetting and drying are the two processes required to block your granny squares, which will improve their ability to maintain their shape well enough. Sprinkle water on your granny squares, or let them sit in water for a little while. After that, spread them on your blocking board, cardboard, or foam mat to dry, pinning the corners of the squares to ensure they dry straight.

Granny Square Patterns

Classic Granny Square

This pattern is the most fundamental among the other granny square patterns and makes granny squares that sit flat and nice, making it ideal for beginners. Chain 3 spacing is used to keep the corners square rather than rounded. The DC stitch, slip stitch, and chain stitch is all you'll need to crochet this pattern.

For this pattern, we would start the granny square using the **chain stitching the center ring** method discussed earlier. However, you can choose to start with any of the three methods discussed.

Remember:

To create the granny square's classic pattern, you'd use the DC cluster, popularly called the granny square cluster, consisting of 3 DCs (double crochet) made within the same space/ gap. The granny clusters are separated by a chain 1 space along its sides and chain 3 spaces/ gaps at the 4 corners. However, I'll demonstrate how to crochet the classic pattern from four rounds of DC clusters and worked in the chain spaces.

Below are the instructions for making the classic granny square pattern.

Steps

Foundation Ring

The granny square should be started with a center ring

1. Chain 4, inserting your hook in the initial chain stitch (the first stitch) after making four chain stitches. After that, the chain stitches should be joined together to form a circle/ring.

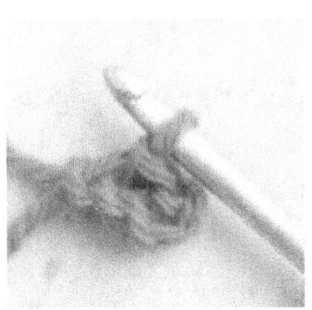

First Round

Below are the instructions for making the granny square's first round.

1. Chain 3; this is counted as the first granny cluster's first DC stitch.
2. 2 DC stitches should be worked in the center ring. There should be what appears to be three parallel DC (the first of the granny clusters), then chain 3.

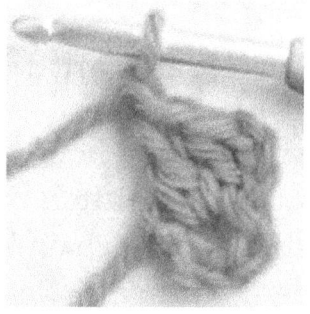

Round 1's first granny cluster being crocheted

3. At this point, the next granny cluster (the second) should be created. 3 DC should be worked in the center ring, then chain 3.
4. Now, create cluster number 3 by working 3 DC in center ring, then chain 3
5. Again, create cluster number 4 by working 3 DC in the center ring, then chain 3.

47

6. There should be four granny clusters presently, each isolated from the next by chain 3 spaces/ gaps at the corners and the end. A slip stitch should be made in the first chain 3's top for the round to be joined and the square's shape to be formed. This concludes round 1.

The first round being completed using a slip stitch

Second Round

1. Chain 4. (The first DC and chain 1 gap/ space are counted as chain 4)

2. 3 DC, chain 3, 3 DC, and chain 1 should be worked in that order in the subsequent chain 3 gap/ space (the 1st corner space).
3. Step 2 should be repeated for an additional 2x, making it 3x in total.
4. 3 DC, 3 chain, and 2 DC should be worked in that order in the final chain 3 gap/ space.
5. The just completed step above should be joined to the third chain of the starting/ beginning chain stitches using a slip stitch. This concludes round 2.

The second round being completed

Third round

1. Chain 3 (this is counted as 1 DC)
2. 2 DC and chain 1 should be worked directly beneath the chain 1 gap/ space of the preceding round, thus creating this round's first granny cluster.
3. 3 DC, chain 3, 3 DC, and then chain 1 should be worked in the subsequent chain 3 corner gap/ space.
4. 3 DC and chain 1 should be worked in the subsequent chain 1 gap/ space.
5. Steps 3-4 should be repeated all over the starting chain. Then afterward, a slip stitch

should be used in joining it to the starting chain 3's top. This concludes round 3.

The third round being completed

Fourth round

1. Chain 4 (this is counted as 1 DC and the chain 1 gap/ space)
2. 3 DC and chain 1 should be worked in the subsequent chain 1 gap/ space.
3. 3 DC, chain 3, 3 DC, and chain 1 should be worked in the subsequent chain 3 corner gap/ space.

4. Step 2-3 should be repeated in every of the other chain 1 and 3 gaps/ spaces
5. 2 DC should be worked in the final chain1 gap/ space.
6. Then afterward, a slip stitch should be used in joining it to the starting chain 3's top. This concludes round 4.

The fourth round being completed

Your granny square could be as large as you'd wish by adding extra rounds. The third and fourth rounds should be repeated as many times as you desire if you want to make your squares large, and ensure to fasten the ends of your yarn tail when you are done and have them weaved in.

Solid Granny Square

This granny square pattern is amongst the widely used granny square variation and is formed using a stitch pattern that results in a square-solid-like appearance. They are often crocheted using only one yarn color, making it ideal if you want a more simplistic style.

They're solid granny squares that have open corners and ones without gaps. I have experimented with several patterns, but my preferred choice is the pattern discussed subsequently, whose corners have aesthetic spaces.

Note:

- Except otherwise stated, the chain stitches at the start of the rounds are considered a stitch.
- For every DC stitch, three chain stitches are used. If this feels loose for you, then chain 2 should be used.

Steps

Foundation ring

To create a ring, chain 5 and use a slip stitch to join (more like starting the granny square using method 2 earlier discussed). Alternatively, the magic ring method can be used.

First Round

1. Chain 3 (this is considered double crochet both here and for the entire pattern)
2. 1 DC and 2 chain should be worked into the ring.

3. 3 DC and 2 chain should be worked into the ring 3 times.
4. 1 DC should be worked and joined using a slip stitch at the beginning chain's top. [12 stitches, Four chain 2 spaces].
5. An extra slip stitch should be made in the chain 2 space (the corner space/ gap)

Second round

1. Chain 3 (this is considered double crochet)
2. 1 DC, 2 chain, and 2 DC should be worked in the subsequent chain 2 space (the corner space/ gap).
3. 1 DC should be worked in every DC along the side and 2 DC, chain 2, and 2 DC should be worked in the chain 2 space corner. This should be repeated for the subsequent two sides.

4. For step 4, do the following;

- Work a DC into the last side's DC.
- 1 DC should be worked in the preceding round's slip stitch.
- 1 DC should be worked in the subsequent preceding round's slip stitch (the one that went in the corner space/ gap.)
- A slip stitch should be used to join the beginning chain's top. [28 stitches, four chain 2 spaces]

5. An extra slip stitch should be made in the chain 2 space (the corner space/ gap)

Note:

If you're experiencing difficulties determining the exact stitch count, ensure you are not mistakenly omitting each side's first DC. This stitch can occasionally be masked by the stitches worked into the corner space/ gap. To identify the starting (first stitch) stitch on each side, the stitches that were worked into the corner space/ gap should be pulled back.

Also, the final DC of this round (round 2) should be worked in the preceding round's slip stitch

Keep repeating this pattern until your desired granny square size is reached.

Third round

Round 2 should be repeated [44 stitches, four chan 2 spaces/ gaps]

Fourth round

Round 2 should be repeated [60 stitches, four chain 2 spaces/ gaps]

Fifth round

Round 2 should be repeated [76 stitches, four chain 2 spaces/ gaps]

Sixth round

Round 2 should be repeated [92 stitches, four chain 2 spaces/ gaps]

Seventh round

Round 2 should be repeated [108 stitches, four chain 2 spaces/ gaps]

Finishing

The yarn should be snipped, fastened off, and the ends weaved in after the granny square has reached the desired size. If there is still a hole in the center, you can close it up with the starting yarn tail.

So there you have it! You've completed your solid granny square.

Sunburst Granny Square

This gorgeous and timeless sunflower-themed sunburst granny square is ideal for beginner-intermediate-level crocheters. Each round of this pattern is worked in a completely different color. Although the sunflower granny square pattern can be made using the colors brown, gold, cream, and yellow to give it a natural sunburst appearance, you can use any colors you wish. However, ensure your yarn is bright in color so your stitches can be seen clearly, and also ensure your stitches are counted while crocheting to avoid losing your position.

Steps

First Round

1. Start off your granny square using a magic ring, or use any of the methods discussed earlier.
2. After that, chain 3 (considered as the first double crochet) and 15 extra DC should be worked into the ring. A slip stitch should be used to join these extra DCs to the top of chain 3's starting/beginning stitch (stitch count of 16 stitches). Cut the yarn and fasten it off.

Second Round

A slip stitch should be used in joining the new yarn to any dc. Chain 2 and work a puff stitch in the same stitch and into every surrounding DC, joining to the first puff stitch, using a slip stitch. (16 puff stitches). Cut the yarn and fasten it off.

To work a puff stitch;

1. Yo, and ensure the hook is inserted in the designated stitch, pulling a loop up (the hook should have 3 loops).
2. Yo, and ensure the hook is inserted in the same stitch, pulling a loop up (the hook should have 5 loops.

3. Yo, and ensure the hook is inserted in the same stitch, pulling a loop up (the hook should have 7 loops.
4. Yo, pulling the yarn across all the hook's loops and fastening off the stitch with chain 1.

Third Round

1. A new yarn should be joined into any chain 1 space using a slip stitch, then chain 2.

We will now work a round of cluster stitches. The round's first cluster stitch is slightly different to give rise to the starting chain.

For the first cluster stitch to be worked, do the following;

2. *Yo and ensure the hook is inserted in the same stitch; Yo, pulling a loop up, Yo again, pulling across 2 loops
3. The above step should be repeated twice
4. The hook should have 4 loops; Yo, pulling across the 4 loops to end the stitch, then chain 2.

The remaining cluster stitches should then be crocheted: work (cluster stitch, chain 2) in the subsequent chain 1 space and into every chain 1 space surrounding it; then, a slip stitch should be used to join them to the starting cluster stitch. (16 cluster stitches). Snip the yarn, and fasten it off.

Below is how to work a cluster stitch for this project if you're still confused;

1. Yo, and ensure the hook is inserted in the designated space, pulling a loop up (the hook should have 3 loops). Yo again, pulling across 2 loops (the hook should have 2 loops)
2. Yo, and ensure the hook is inserted in the same space/ gap, pulling a loop up. Yo again, pulling across 2 loops (the hook should have 3 loops)

3. Yo, and ensure the hook is inserted in the same space/ gap, pulling a loop up. Yo again, pulling across 2 loops (the hook should have 4 loops)
4. Yo, and ensure the hook is inserted in the same space/ gap, pulling a loop up. Yo again, pulling across 2 loops (the hook should have 5 loops)
5. Yo, pulling the yarn across all the hook's loops

Fourth Round

1. A new yarn should be joined into any chain 2 space using a slip stitch. Chain 4 (considered as the first treble crochet), then 2 treble crochet should be worked in the same space/ gap.
2. Now, the first side should be worked by crocheting 3 DC into the subsequent chain 2

space, 3 HDC into the subsequent chain 2 space, and 3 DC into the subsequent chain 2 space. This constitutes the square's first side.

3. Making the first corner is the next step. To do this, work 3 TR into the subsequent chain 2 space, chain 3 and 3 TR in the same chain 2 space (the 1st corner).

The side and corner procedure will be repeated to create the rest of the sides and corners.

4. The second side should be crocheted by working 3 DC, 3 HDC, and 3 DC into the subsequent chain 2 space.

5. The second corner should be crocheted by working 3 TR into the subsequent chain 2 space, chain 3, and 3 TR in the same chain 2 space

6. The third side should be crocheted by working 3 DC into the subsequent chain 2 space, 3 HDC into the subsequent chain 2 space, and 3 DC into the subsequent chain 2 space.

7. The third corner should be crocheted by working 3 TR into the subsequent chain 2 space, chain 3, and 3 TR in the same chain 2 space.

8. The last side should be crocheted y working 3 DC into the subsequent chain 2 space, 3 HDC into the subsequent chain 2 space, and 3 DC into the subsequent chain 2 space.

9. For the last corner to be completed, 3 TR should be worked in the same space/ gap as the starting treble crochet stitches, chain 3, and ensure a slip stitch is used to join them to the top of chain'4 beginning/ starting stitch.

Finishing

So there you have it! You've completed your sunburst granny square. The yarn should be snipped, fastened off, and the ends weaved in.

Hexagon Granny Square

This granny square is crocheted in similarity to a hexagon but is quite comparable to the traditional/classic granny square pattern. This hexagon pattern has gained a great deal of attention recently and serves as an ideal pattern for crocheting everything from table runners to afghans.

Steps

1. Work a magic ring to begin this pattern, securing it using a stitch.

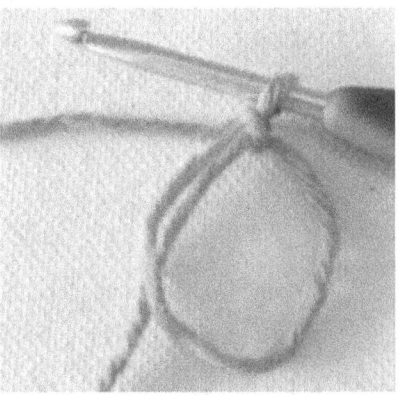

2. Chain 2 (considered as 1 DC), then ensure 1 DC is worked into the ring. *Chain 2 again, then ensure

2 DC is worked into the ring. *Repeat till there are six 2 DC clusters spaced apart by chain 2

3. The tail of the yarn should be pulled to complete the circle, finishing the round using a slip stitch made into your starting chain 2's back loop.

4. Chain 3 (considered 1 DC), then ensure 1 DC is worked in the subsequent stitch.

5. You've now gotten to a corner space/ gap.

   To make the subsequent corner;

   - *1 DC, chain 2, *1 DC should be worked in the space.
   - After that, 1 DC should be worked in every subsequent stitch, working *1 DC, chain 2, *1 DC in every corner space.
   - The round should be joined using a slip stitch made into your starting chain 3's back loop.

6. Do the following;

- Chain 3 (considered as 1 DC), then ensure 1 DC is worked in every of the subsequent stitches.
- *1 DC, chain 2, *1 DC should be worked into every corner space all around, working 1 DC into every stitch.
- Use a slip stitch to complete the round.

7. Repeat step 6 above once again, and you'd have completed your hexagon granny square pattern.

Circle Granny Square

This granny square is similar to a solid granny square, which starts out as a circle before eventually transforming into a square. I adore this pattern and believe it'd look stunning when crocheted into an afghan for your couch, a lap wrap, or a baby blanket. Similar to the traditional classic granny square, there are countless projects for which this pattern can be used for.

Steps

First round

1. Make a magic ring.
2. Chain 3 (considered the first DC), working 11 DCs (12 stitches in total).
3. Join the above step to the beginning chain 3's third chain using a slip stitch.

Second round

1. Chain 3 (considered the first DC)
2. Work a DC in the same stitch as chain 3, and then work 2 DC in every stitch (24 stitches in total).
3. Join the above step to the beginning chain 3's third chain using a slip stitch.

Third round

1. Chain 3 (considered the first DC)
2. Work a DC in the same stitch as chain 3
3. Work another DC into the subsequent stitch
4. Work *2 DC into the subsequent stitch and;
5. Work another 1 DC into the subsequent stitch.
6. Repeat from * to complete (36 stitches in total).
7. Hold off before your final yarn over on the round's final DC, cutting the yarn and yarning over using a new color as seen below.

Fourth round

1. Chain 3 (considered the first DC)
2. Work a DC in the same stitch as chain 3
3. Chain 1, then do the following;

- Work 2 DC into subsequent stitch
- Work a HDC into every of the subsequent 2 stitches
- Work a SC into every of the subsequent 3 stitches
- Work another HDC into every of the subsequent 2 stitches
- Work another *2 DC into the subsequent stitch, then chain 1
- Work another 2 DC into the subsequent stitch
- Work another HDC into every of the subsequent 2 stitches
- Work a SC into every of the subsequent 3 stitches
- Work another HDC into every of the subsequent 2 stitches
- Repeat from * twice.

4. Join the above step to the beginning chain 3's third chain using a slip stitch, slip stitching into the subsequent chain 1 corner space.

Fifth round

1. Chain 3 (considered the first DC)
2. Work a DC, chain 1 and 2 DC into the corner space
3. Work a DC into every stitch till you get to the subsequent corner

The arrows below show the location to crochet the first DC after your corner has been worked.

There should be a total of 11 crocheted stitches at this point along the side of your pattern's straight edge, excluding the stitches at the corners

4. Now, work 2 DC, chain 1, and 2 DC into the corner space. Proceed in this manner till you get to the end of the round
5. Join the above step to the beginning chain 3's third chain using a slip stitch while slip stitching into the subsequent corner space.

Sixth round

1. Chain 3 (considered the first DC)
2. Work a DC, chain 2, and 2 DC into the corner space
3. Work a DC into every stitch till you've gotten to the subsequent corner

There should be a total of 15 crocheted stitches at this point along the side of your pattern's straight edge, excluding the stitches at the corners

4. Now, work 2 DC, chain 2, and 2 DC into the corner space; this procedure should be repeated till you get to the round's end.
5. Join the above step to the starting chain 3's third chain using a slip stitch while slip stitching into the subsequent corner space. Cut the yarn tail, fasten it off and have it weaved in.

The End... Almost!

Hey! This book has come to its last chapter, and I trust you've had a good read thus far.

As a self-published author with a limited advertising budget, I depend on you, my readers, to post a quick review of my book on Amazon because readers hardly post reviews.

So, if you truly liked this book, would you kindly...

Submit a quick review on Amazon by clicking >> here.

Thanks so much.

Eye-Shaped Granny Square

I adore everything about granny squares, and I'm referring to the well-known, traditional/ classic, solid, circle, and hexagon granny squares. And like all the variations already discussed, this eye-shaped granny square has several application areas. A bunch of these granny squares would work for making a tote bag, cushion, or top. The options are limitless.

Note

- Chain 1, chain 2, and chain 3 at the start of a round are counted as 1 SC, 1 HDC, and 1 DC, respectively.
- All color changes should be made in the final two loops of the last stitch of the old/ previous color.

Steps

First round

1. Make a magic ring using your preferred yarn color.

2. Work chain 3 and 11 DC in the magic ring, then join the above step to the starting chain 3's third chain using a slip stitch (12 stitches in total)

Second round

1. Pick up a different yarn color, and work chain 3
2. Work a DC in the same stitch as chain 3
3. Work 2 DC in every stitch across
4. Join the above step to the starting chain 3's third chain using a slip stitch (24 stitches in total)

Third round

1. Pick up a different yarn color, and work chain 3
2. Work a DC in the same stitch as chain 3
3. Work a DC into the subsequent stitch and 2 DC into the subsequent stitch; repeat 11 times
4. Work a DC in the final stitch
5. Join the above step to the starting chain 3's third chain using a slip stitch (36 stitches in total)

Fourth round

1. Pick up a different yarn color, and work chain 3
2. Work a SC into the subsequent stitch
3. Increase and work a SC into every of the subsequent two stitches; repeat 3 times
4. Work a HDC into the subsequent stitch, 2 HDC into the subsequent stitch, and a DC into the subsequent stitch.
5. Work 2 TR into the subsequent stitch. Then work a DC into the subsequent stitch, 2 HDC into the subsequent stitch, and HDC into the subsequent stitch. Finally, work a SC into every of the subsequent two stitches.

6. Increase and work a SC into every of the subsequent two stitches; repeat 3 times.
7. Then work a HDC into the subsequent stitch, 2 HDC into the subsequent stitch, and a DC into the subsequent stitch
8. Finally, work 2 TR into the subsequent stitch, a DC into the subsequent stitch, 2 HDC into the subsequent stitch, and a HDC into the subsequent stitch.
9. Join the above step to the round's first stitch using a slip stitch (48 stitches in total)

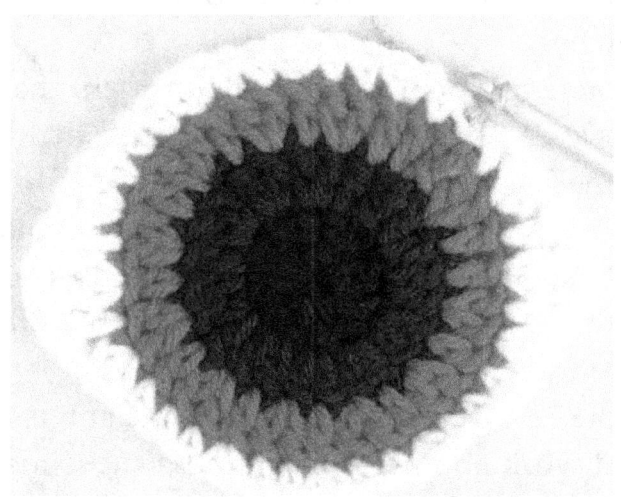

Fifth round

1. Pick up a different yarn color, work chain 2, and HDC into every of the subsequent two stitches; then work a DC into every of the subsequent three stitches.
2. Work 2 TR into the subsequent stitch, chain 2, and work another 2 TR into the subsequent stitch (first corner).
3. Work a DC into every of the subsequent three stitches, HDC into every of the subsequent five stitches, and SC into every of the subsequent two stitches.
4. Work 2 SC into the subsequent stitch, chain 2, and work 2 SC into the subsequent stitch (second corner)
5. Work a SC into every of the subsequent two stitches, HDC into every of the subsequent five stitches, and DC into every of the subsequent three stitches.
6. Work 2 TR into the subsequent stitch, chain 2, and work another 2 TR into the subsequent stitch (third corner).
7. Work a DC into every of the subsequent three stitches, HDC into every of the subsequent five

stitches, and SC into every of the subsequent two stitches.

8. Work 2 SC into the subsequent stitch, chain 2, and work 2 SC into the subsequent stitch (fourth corner)

9. Work a SC into every of the subsequent two stitches and HDC into every of the subsequent five stitches.

10. Join the above step to the starting chain 2's second chain using a slip stitch (54 stitches and 4 chain-2 corner spaces in total)

11. Don't fasten off

Sixth round

1. Chain 2, work HDC into every of the subsequent seven stitches, then work the stitches below 3 times

   - 2 HDC, chain 1, and 2 HDC in the corner space.
   - HDC into every of the subsequent 14 stitches.

2. Work HDC into every of the other six stitches

3. Join the above step to the starting chain 2's second chain using a slip stitch (72 stitches and 4 chain-2 corner spaces in total)

Seventh round

1. Pick up a different yarn color and work chain 1.
2. Work SC into every of the subsequent nine stitches, then work the stitches below 3 times

    *   2 SC into the corner space and SC into every of the subsequent 18 stitches.

3. Work 2 SC into the corner space
4. Work SC into every of the subsequent 8 stitches.
5. Join the above step to the starting/ beginning round's first chain using a slip stitch (80 stitches in total).
6. Now fasten your yarn tail and weave the ends in.